On Authorship:

Essays on the Emotional Realities of Being a Professional Writer

By
Martin Vidal

Table of Contents

Preface v
I. How Writers Are Made...1
II. Why Writing Takes Courage 7
III. Why You Can't Force Yourself To Write 13
IV. Why It's So Hard to Succeed as a Writer................................19
V. How to Deal With Being a Broke Writer.................................25
VI. Why the People Closest to You Might Not Love Your Writing..........................31
VII. Should a Writer Be a Person or a Brand?.............................37
VIII. Is It Egotistical to Post Your Writings?...............................43
IX. Why Your Writing Might Be Too Good to Be Popular.......49
X. Why Having the Courage to Be Authentic Is the Key to Success 55
XI. Why You Should Write Less..61
XII. Why You Should Care Less About Your Writing 65
XIII. Why Reading Is Essential for Writers.................................73
XIV. How Writing Heals Trauma..79
In Conclusion..87
Notes 89

Preface

I view writing as a spiritual exercise, and I believe anyone else who truly loves the craft feels the same. However, limited on time as we are, what we love for its own sake often finds itself at odds with what we must make time for, in order to meet the demands of necessity and to lead a pragmatic existence. Thus, when someone truly loves to write, they tend to find themselves trying to meld these two draws on their time: They try to turn their passion into their profession, by becoming professional writers. This transition is fraught with emotional consequences. How to force oneself to write on deadlines and for broad appeal, how to make private writings public, and how to promote that writing thereafter can often work to pervert a beloved practice into something quite different. As I walked this divide, I encountered many challenges and personal questions, which inspired me to write about them, in order to develop a thoughtful approach to the problems presented and to express what I was feeling all the while. In the end, I believe this collection of essays will speak to the heart of any who have a deep love for the art of writing. Any other type of artist is also likely to find that my experiences relate well to their own. To that end, I offer in one place a collection of my essays on the subject, in the form of this work, *On Authorship*.

I

How Writers Are Made

Writers are formed in solitude

Writing is a practice that requires solitude. It is, in essence, a conversation without the requisite of a second party. Just as we can only carry on a conversation with one person at a time—even if we occasionally alternate between two or more—this conversation, too, precludes all others while active. In other words, it is to be done alone. This fact suggests that any who prefer this art, prefer also to spend a great deal of their time in isolation.

The young politician finds they have the gift of gab, and swims through any social setting with ease, so their mind is made up for them. Their constitution has determined that here lie their talents and inclinations, and if they are to provide value, as we all must, then this career shall be their chief aspiration. Dreams are born, not made.

The young writer, instead, is either ostracized or self-ostracized. Frankly, society doesn't expend much effort in distinguishing between the two, and any non-participant is to a degree shunned as a matter of course. By choice or circumstance, they find themselves in a society of one.

One carries so much trauma that their mind is filled with painful memories, and finding the content of their thinking life too difficult to voice, and the average person uninterested in hearing it, they express it by writing. Another may have been bullied and rejected as a child, or had social anxiety, or moved from place to place and was therefore unable to make close friends, or had any of a thousand other reasons why they simply could not express themselves to the people around them. The writing itself begins to happen, as an organic function, before words are ever typed or written. The writing is only the externalized form of what are monologues and imaginings occurring in the mind left to its own devices. This lone, churning mind has the wants of any other, and it must express. It finds that the page is an eager listener.

The writer necessarily lives a life on the fringe. They are an outcast, an oddity—a stray sheep. Perhaps if sharks or reptiles were made as intelligent as humans, they'd all be writers, but this is not the case, so we find instead an exception to the rule in an anti-social individual amid a social species. They are not only made to be alone but lonely, for whatever malfunction keeps them from fitting in with the crowd, they are still not so neatly organized as to be without the want of friendship, socialization, and a sense of belonging. There is a tension in their soul.

Finding themselves excluded, they have wants left unfulfilled. They must express, and the page allows them to do so. Writing, in turn, becomes a subtle relief. This is how one first comes to like writing. However, what seems to really make a writer is when one comes to see the craft as a ticket back to the place from which they were barred. Somebody comes across the work of the young writer and gives it genuine praise. Suddenly, the path back to the center is lighted, and they see how a society they never felt at home in might come to value them. Now, they begin to work from the fringe for access to the center. This is how writing goes from hobby to career, from casual to consuming.

The writer, as an archetype, is a moral exile. Any good writer must live up to that description. Society is a collection of minds. Those minds feed into one another, by imitating and building off of each other, until they form a single body. The writer is a cell of society separated from that body. This isolated portion is no longer subject to the impulses of that larger mass. Its feeling and intellectual forces are left to work in a direction diverging from that of the commons. Yet, that inner tension makes it so that the writer, even as an outsider, is still hungrily looking in; their social wants are exercised through an eager observance in the place of actual involvement. In many ways, writers are more social-minded than their socially active counterparts. They become, for this reason, society's mirrors, analysts, and instructors.

Writers are a powerful force in the social environment. Society is a reactive tissue. Even in the most liberal of democracies, there is hardly any freedom on the part of the individual when woven into the social tapestry. With every interaction, society doles out reward for adhering to its expectations or exacts punishment for failing to. No person is so tireless that they won't sooner or later revert to the path of least resistance; there is no resisting society without escaping it. The populations of this world are something like bodies of water—who can float on the ocean and not rise or fall with the waves and tides?

However, as society is nothing more than the product of working minds, the lone mind performs this same function and builds a society within itself. As it is not bound by what is, it grants visions of a world that could be. This castoff paints a picture of the city as seen from outside its walls, and those within learn from it their true place in the world. The stray sheep becomes the shepherd. Thus, the writer is fully formed.

The immigrant from a far-off land sees their new country with eyes for things the lifelong citizen takes for granted. The true writer is a person without a land, who carries with them a culture of their own creation, only tangentially related to the one they are themselves a product of. To lament that one feels somewhat of a foreigner, even among close friends and family, is to grab hold of the sharp side of a powerful tool; opposite this is an ability for seeing past the myopia of the maze, for looking upon the whole that lies beyond the hedge enveloping the individual on all sides.

Still, a writer, like any other person, is a dichotomy. They have forward facing eyes, and opposite them are those that face inward. Thinking and writing in solitude doesn't only work to render transparent the externals; it allows for the unfurling of the internal as well. We are enclosed in a maze and have another enclosed within us. If we take for granted our cultural milieu because it is and always has been constantly present, imagine how blind we are to the particulars of our self. We've never once stepped outside the boundaries of our being and have no other soul to employ as an object for comparison. The universe within is every bit as illimitable as the one without; it is an infinity and requires an eternity to explore. All the years of our lives don't amount to a fraction of what would be needed, and those who are constantly distracted by the scenes of society will only ever catch a glimpse of themselves.

The first obligation of the writer is to look at the world and speak honestly about what they see. The second obligation is to look in themselves and do the same. There are two sides to individual existence: the inside and the out, the self and all else. The fresh perspective, earned in isolation, must be applied to both. When it gives a picture of the world, it teaches of a new world; when it gives a picture of the soul, it reveals the old soul. An unvarnished individual ceases to be individual; in our truest essence, we are all one and the same. To tap into this is to cross all dividing lines, transcend the particular, and enter the universal. If we can bravely reveal ourselves, we will reveal to all others themselves in turn.

By the law of universal balance, which ensures any subtraction from one side of the scale will be met by an addition to the opposing side, even exile has its benefits. For every ounce of suffering, the outcast is granted an equal portion of power by their externalized vantage point.

Give of your world, and give of your self, young writer. It is the most valuable thing in the world.

II

Why Writing Takes Courage

Making your writing public can be nerve-wracking, but the feeling is justified

I, like you, feel a qualm of anxiety every time I go to make a piece of writing public. I wanted to explore this feeling, learn what underlies that fear, and determine whether or not it's warranted. What I've realized is that to be a writer takes a tremendous amount of courage.

The paper confessional

A writer implicates themselves by pointing to realities that they could only be aware of by having experienced them or dwelt on them. To write about envy, infidelity, addiction, fear, failure, love, or any number of the other messy things that make up life as we know it, is invariably to confess to the world that you have experienced such things and how. Writing is public confession.

When you first meet a person, there is an understanding that a certain level of comfort must develop between the two of you before any real intimacy can be had, and so one's personal feelings and experiences are tucked away for a time. Yet, these thoughts and sentiments are displayed for all the world in our writing—and would be on billboards if we were afforded the opportunity. It takes courage to be this vulnerable.

Even when dealing with the most sterile subjects, the impressionability of words, which offers a million ways to say a single thing, captures the slightest attendant sentiment, so that an author's opinion can never truly be hidden, for the selection of one adjective over another, the particularly inspired metaphor, the unusually incisive insight, or simply one word too many, communicates an appreciation of one line of thinking over another. It is impossible to conceal passion in writing.

Flying blind

Writing intensifies the social realities we all face just by participating in society: never getting to see yourself through the eyes of others, guessing at the veracity of your self-assessments, and always wondering if you're sufficiently adequate and well-received. The words that criticize always seem so much more credible than those that compliment.

I've joked with friends that I'd believe myself to be an excellent writer only if I won a Pulitzer, but, truthfully, if that impossibility ever became reality, I think I'd be more likely to question the merit of the bestowal. I've often wished for such a horrid thing as a devil on my back constantly pointing out everything wrong in my writing, as it would be preferable to the inescapable ignorance.

There is a far-sightedness inherent in human nature, so that all that is closest to us is blurred. We can never be unbiased judges of our competence, intelligence, social reception, etc. Anyone who has ever watched one of those televised singing competitions has seen just how self-deluded a person can be, how they can believe themselves the best singer in the world, when all the world sees just how talentless they are. Any artist with open eyes, including writers, must always consider this to possibly be the case for themselves, for there are no objective measures of skill when it comes to pursuits such as these.

Opening the vault

Every writer first feels the draw to put pen to paper as a sort of refuge. The blank, silent page and the obedient pen accept our thoughts without judgment and retain them faithfully. To make one's work public is to allow every stranger with a passing curiosity access to that most sacred place.

Packaging personhood

The only thing an author has to give are the products of their private life. The thoughts and emotions that consume us, the experiences that change us, and everything else concealed in that fortress of the mind is spilled out onto a page for general consumption. What is more representative of who you are as a person than these things?

Words are vessels that writers fill with their thoughts, memories, and emotions, and ship off to whomever will have them. An author bottles their doubts, boxes their delights, and packages their pain, and then sells them like a shopkeeper. We are peddlers of our own personhood.

A carpenter, cleaner, or lawyer can claim without a care that they provide the best service, just as many a salesman can boast freely about the quality of their product. But the world will never abide a writer making claims of their own greatness: It is too central to who one is. To say "I am a masterful writer" is far too egotistical a claim; it is akin to saying, "I am amazingly beautiful" or "I am incredibly smart"—these things strike too close to the core of our being. It is as if to say, "I am an admirable person." This exemplifies just how personal a written work is.

Moreover, there is a vulnerability in effort, in demonstrating one's capability; writing is by no means an exception to this. To the burden of baring one's soul, we add the difficulty that it must also be done skillfully. A sentence containing a heartfelt sentiment and a profound observation is rendered powerless by a conspicuous typo.

The difficulty of communication

There are a great many challenges involved in the skill of writing. There are thousands of words to be memorized, each with a variety of definitions and connotations; there is granular detail in the rules of grammar, as finely honed as would be expected for any craft as essential and ancient as writing; and there are multifarious, inscrutable forms of eloquence and style; but the most difficult part of writing is not to say a thing exactly right but to predict exactly how it is most likely to be read.

Good writing is an unusually empathetic exercise. One must master and organize their own thoughts to write well, but one must also peer into the unknowable mind of their reader. This is the difficulty of communication, and it is central to the art of writing.

The reach of words

Silent writing echos longer and carries farther than the loudest shout. A sentence can make its way around the world. A configuration of words can be reproduced by a million tongues. The words one writes today might be read for millennia to follow, and this daunting reality is something that writers not only face but that they pray for. There is an intrepid bravery in being a writer that none but those who have this calling can understand.

A commitment to permanence

To write is to make a record of one's sentiments. There is nowhere to hide in writing. A written work is unchanging and unresponsive. What it says is what it says until the end of time. We may change, but what we've written is set in stone. Every word we make public is as much an indelible mark on our reputation as a tattoo is upon the skin.

The impossibility of originality

There is a constantly present feeling that every word I write has been said before, and that I am less a person than an echo. Billions of people produce words everyday. Billions of people produced words before I ever formed my first. A sort of unwitting plagiarism is not the exception when writing but the rule.

A writer must grapple directly with the redundancy of humanity. Those that take up this calling are no more reiterations and repetitions of their predecessors than those in any other field, but because the works of those who came before us remain so active and well-preserved, they contend with us for attention throughout our lives.

Just the other day I wrote that, "There is no skill in navigating calm waters." Two days later I stumbled across a quote of FDR's: "A smooth sea never made a skilled sailor."[1] He said this not only before I was born but before either of my parents were born. My attempt at originality was precluded long before I drew my first breath. And when people read this text, they will to a person prefer the former President's words over my own. And why shouldn't they? Who am I compared to him? Only writers are truly haunted by ghosts of the past.

The overwhelming odds

Writing is such an essential skill that it is practiced by everyone. There is scarcely a comparable profession wherein one is expected to outperform every modern person. The craftsmen need only compete with the fellows in their field, and the retailers each have a product with a niche. There is a democracy to writing that doesn't exist for other skills. Anyone can write, and anyone can make it public. With all the world competing to be heard, how will your voice rise above the clamor? To be a successful writer is among the most audacious of dreams.

Conclusion

Is it any wonder that the word "masochism" is named after a novelist, Leopold von Sacher-Masoch?[2] The next time you get that thrill of anxiety when making your work public, remember this: That feeling is warranted. You have just done an incredibly brave thing.

Come what may, you took a bold leap.

III

Why You Can't Force Yourself To Write

Inspiration doesn't come on command

Writer's block is a silly concept. If one doesn't feel the motivation to put pen to paper, if they are not overtaken by ideas and a flow of words, why write? Like most forced things, writing under these circumstances is only done for money. Writer's block is a symptom of careerism.

Art is like public service; it must be done for the right reasons or not at all. Manual labor can and should be forced. The worker is measured by a different strain of virtue. Sore limbs and sweat dripping from the brow evidence a strong determination to work. However, the artist, philanthropist, and public servant are exactly the opposite. If not carried here on the breeze, if the soul did not pull you hither almost unconsciously, then this is not the place for you.

The true virtue of art is that it is egoless, and will is to ego as branch is to trunk. Thus, art cannot be willed. We do not convince ourselves to have an appetite for beauty, or to love those cherished persons in our lives; these wants simply come over us like a hunger. Just as we have a voluntary and involuntary nervous system, the actions performed by every individual fall into one of these two categories: Sometimes in life we must muster our strength to raise the axe or bury the spade, but creativity is as unconscious as a heartbeat or a breath. Sometimes one pushes, and at other times, they are pushed. There are mechanical demonstrations of effort, and there are sprightly demonstrations of non-effort. Writing must be a non-effort. To quote a friend, it is "a suspension of effort rather than an effort in itself."

If anything, the urge to create is often overpowering, leaving us without a choice. It might strike just as one is trying to fall asleep, and the mind will not rest now that it has honed in on some idea it is eager to work on. Having inspiration pull us by the hand in this manner is the only suitable way to create. If instead we look at our wants laid out before us as if on a grocery list, and say, "I wish to be famous and celebrated and paid this amount, and so I will try to write to accomplish this," then we will go looking for inspiration, and it will hide from us. We will tug at it and find that it refuses to come. When we have managed to yank it forth a bit, that airy creature will come forward shriveled, broken, and disfigured. Inspiration only ever plays the part of master. We can put out feed for the birds, yes, and hope they will come, but if we capture and cage them, they lose the marvelous power of freedom that first drew us to them. A wing in confinement is a useless thing. To try and force the process of creativity is like housing the wind; it becomes changed and stagnant a moment later.

To write for money alone is to write for an audience. There is hardly a bigger mistake the writer can make. If I were to try to tell you what it is you want to hear, to be equipped for the task I should come to know you better than you know yourself. Even with the people I am closest to, I find that though I often stand before them and look directly at their face, their personhood remains enclosed behind it—I am turned away at the gates. I would be lost if attempting to write for my familiars, so how am

I to write for strangers? The writer is bound to a single circumference: the border of their being. I have only my existence and my experiences to offer. I would do better to explore the labyrinth inside myself; perhaps, I will come across something that even I am surprised to find, and bringing that forward, see if it reveals to you some similar and secreted thing tucked away inside yourself. I know very little about what you might want to read, but I know absolutely what it is I want to say, and it is far more becoming to keep at being an expert in this subject than a novice at any other.

What a grotesque picture sycophancy makes in all quarters. When we are overly deferential to another person we sell ourselves cheaply. What power does master wield over servant that the latter should disregard all of their opinions and inclinations in order to express a complete agreement with the former? It is unsightly for any person to attempt at playing the part of another's shadow when the grandeur of existence is equally present in both parties. Cowardice and obsequiousness are the worst forms of rejection of self. There is a selflessness at the heart of masterful writing, but this removal of self is for the sake of allowing the entrance of some higher power. Whatever that magical inspiration might be properly called, it is something godly, something with the mien of spirituality. The elements of the metaphysical—Truth, Beauty, and Goodness—flow into the artist when they have been made an empty vessel. This alone is a worthy reason to disregard one's self. If instead we put aside our wants and natural calling to attempt and satisfy another mortal, we trade our person in full for a motley of parts belonging to others. If one writes just for an audience, they put themselves aside to let a hideous chimera stand in their place; a complete and homogenous whole is exchanged for the eyes of one and the ears of another, informed by criticisms here and assorted praise there, so that the road crooks so sharply from one direction to another that it cannot attain one of the essential features of good writing: a smooth, consistent movement from one line and one paragraph to the next.

The only worthy motivation of a writer is self-destruction. The true trajectory of creativity is to spend one's days working at every minor detail in a piece until it has been deemed complete; then, to love it for five minutes and bask in the appreciation shown to it by others for a day or two; and, finally, to hate it. The foundation of optimism is an unbalanced scale; it is a prejudice against the past. Let yesterday be tainted so that tomorrow might shine brighter. That is the self-defeating hunger of genius. If it has been completed, it must necessarily be inferior when compared to whatever is to come next. To strive to create a masterpiece is the mark of brilliance; to create a masterpiece is the mark of death. When the peak has been reached and only the descent remains, what is left in the art?

This self-destruction is a rainbow of many shades. The urge to overcome one's past self, by superseding each creation with another, is an instinct felt even by the earliest aspirant. True mastery, however, is found in the self-destruction of the present. Ego is the enemy of art. The aspiring author learns thousands and thousands of words; studies the rules of grammar down to the smallest nuance; and practices alliteration, assonance, chiasmus, and all other varieties of literary construction. They look at the greats and hope to have a style of writing on par with theirs. They don't want to write; they want to be a writer. But the magic was never in the words, or sounds, or elegant arrangements; it was in the soul hiding behind it all. Skill only serves to aid in its expression. If one asks us to look at how prettily they string words together, we are repulsed by it. But if in those words they show us pain or pleasure, beauty or struggle, faith or pride, then we are mesmerized.

Every artist is a glazier. The master of all craftspeople is she who makes windows. No one ever approaches a window in a home and says to themselves, *What a beautiful piece of glass*. Instead, they look through it and into the world. To write, or paint, or sing, or build, or speak, is to create a window. You have no interest in what it is I have to say, and I have no interest in what it is you would say. It is when we can see the sunset in a sonnet, or feel the tremble of love from a story, or recognize our own pain in another's, that we are taken into something sublime.

We are often made insecure by another writer's facility with words and capacity for description. Pretty words are, indeed, pretty. However, it is not a command of the language that gives a piece of writing any worth; its only real value is in the truths conveyed within. And truth doesn't belong to skill so much as courage, so much as self-destruction. Skillful writing is but rose petals on the outward path; courage is what carries the truth forward. Here I am, shoddy and undecorated, and this shabby figure is the most glorious, for it is not the glitter that makes a writer but the ground. Are they connected to all things? Have they been honest? Honesty is a method of transfer; it is a vehicle and a bridge. An honest word brings reality to wherever it is spoken. The sky appears as blue, a dog chases its tail, and a man is ashamed of his failings; whatever at all that is true, that is of the universe. The truth was here before we found it. We are not its creators, only its messengers—only the window makers. To speak truth, then, is to put one's self aside. This is art, and this is the only reason to write.

If the truth will not obey us today, if beauty is feeling shy and skittish, and goodness hides in a fog, we have nothing to give. We must put down our pen and walk away. We are not enough on our own. Fortunately, the oversoul is all around us, and if we stop flailing about after it, that metaphysical cloud will fill in the still air around us. Let inspiration come when it will—we have no other choice.

IV

Why It's So Hard to Succeed as a Writer

Few things are more difficult to promote than writers and their works

There are a lot of obvious barriers to success as a writer. For one, there's already a mile of text out there for every available inch of attention span. For another, it's rare to have to compete with those that live up the street *and* those that died a thousand years ago on some faraway continent. Good writing is immortal, and I'm not sure I'll ever be able to make a strong argument for someone reading my work over La Rochefoucauld's. Yet, beyond all the conditions that exist out in the world, the reasons why most writers fail can be found in the very nature of writing.

What makes a writer

When I was young (and, to a lesser degree, even in the present) I had terrible social anxiety. Eye contact would send a shock through me, and talking to people was a little bit like touching the stove. My mouth was plenty good for eating food with, and I could smile as well as the rest, but it was useless for getting words out. A soul needs a mouth; I needed to express.

When I was in elementary school, I was given my first creative writing assignment, and my hand ran wild: We were asked to take 30 minutes to write a paragraph starting with "I found an egg in the yard...", but I wrote three pages and only stopped because we hit our time limit. It had all been bottled up inside, so it rushed out of me. The teacher loved what I wrote and told me so. I was dismayed when she insisted on reading it to the class; I hid in the bathroom while she did.

Years later, when I was about 9 years old, another teacher would accuse me of plagiarizing a poem. After being unable to find the supposed "original," she insisted some adult must've written it for me, as it was too good to have been written by a child. It gave me a shock at the time, and my anxious heart raced till I was breathless, but as the fear died down, I felt proud. Unintended though it was, I had never before received such a grand compliment. After that incident, writing moved from being something I liked doing to something that felt connected to my worth as an individual. Every tool in the toolbox has its use, and writing felt like mine. I often hear stories like this from other writers as well.

Writing is lonely. It can be tedious. What we write is apt to fall short of what we want it to be. Writers certainly aren't regarded as society's stars. We're expected to be both pompous and poor—a rare combination, really. Why would anyone want to be a writer? I proffer that we write only ever as a second choice. One thing or another has worked to bar us from the world of social butterflies and cocksure gascons. Writing is a type of echo chamber, wherein the individual in isolation can, in a very real way, talk to themselves. We were forced from a place where we so wanted to belong and left without an outlet for that most human need: to express. Writing gave us a vent for expression; it, then, offered us an opportunity for redemption. It offered us a semblance of self-worth when we could find it nowhere else. That is the common journey I've heard of, over and over again, from different writers. Writing is an anti-social solution to a social want. The blank page is an ear to listen, and a mouth to speak back to us, when there is no other.

Show me a writer who isn't also a reader. How many days of our lives have we spent in what seems like complete isolation, when in fact we've been eagerly conversing with an unmet friend? If only you knew the conversations I've had with Nietzsche, or how engrossed I am when my old pal Dostoyevsky sets about telling stories! On a Friday night, it's expected that one would be found with friends at home or at a bar, and to many it seems an oddity that one should instead be alone with a book. Well, what you call spending time with friends is truly time spent talking, that is, trading words. My friends bequeathed me their words before their passing, and I've laughed, and quarreled, and been inspired by affection in response to my friends' words, just as you have with yours—I daresay my friends had more to say.

At base, the entire social tapestry consists of words. Lovers fall into each other's arms following an exchange of romantic phrases, business deals are settled after swapping technical terms, and friends know each other only as well as the syllables they've shared. Brotherhood is a type of banter, and love is its own language. Words are as elemental to relationships as hydrogen and oxygen are to the clouds and the oceans. If we didn't have a need to communicate with one another, we would've never needed them at all. But nature has designed us so that this tool is a part of who we are. The caged bird still flaps its wings, the fish stranded on dry land undulates its body in an attempt to swim, and the person in isolation makes words.

Promotion

Business is an inherently social enterprise. There is no such thing as commerce in isolation. There are, of course, extroverted writers, but they're something like day-walking vampires: a rarity or half-breed at best. And the bulk of the overlap, between extroversion and a propensity for writing, is found in those who have pursued some career in this or that field and chose to write as an extension of it. But among those who are first and foremost drawn to the quiet, solitary, pensive act, there is seldom a socially inclined individual to be found.

Being a writer is very much given to being anti-social. Being a successful writer, however, is not. Society measures success in terms of fame, prestige, and wealth. Character, skill, and health are personal measures of success, but dreams of achieving these things rarely rouse the passions. Success, as we commonly conceive of it, is achieved by social means. Wealth is a function of commerce, fame is a measure of how many people recognize one's name, and prestige is but a mound of opinions. The degree to which one succeeds at these things is determined by headcount. She is more famous who has been spoken of by 1,000 and 1 people than whomever is known by only a 1,000.

If the writer is to have any success, they must make frequent forays out into the bustling world they've become so adept at avoiding. Though they are by nature withdrawn, they must assume a role reminiscent of a rock star. One must give lectures, attend book signings and readings, do interviews, etc. All of these occasions of social interaction, personal divulgence, and events where one is the center of attention are necessary ingredients to a thriving career as an author. It is incredibly difficult to reach the point where it is even an option to hold events such as these. Only a smattering of writers ever achieve this status, and though they worked to exhaustion to make it possible, to what extent must they go against their personal instincts just to keep it going? Success as a writer often means going against the grain of one's being and swimming upstream against the currents of the soul.

A written work is inherently difficult to profit from. No matter how enlightening a book one writes, they won't find a reader who needs, for themselves, more than one copy. We need food daily, and new clothes annually, but a book lasts a lifetime. Once you have sold a person your work, there is no opportunity to sell it to them again. When we have gotten it into one set of hands, we must find another set of hands. To have any real hope of finding a repeat customer, the author must have at least two books to sell.

Moreover, writing doesn't lend itself to promotion. Isn't the best writing a nuanced picture of the soul? Isn't every masterpiece abounding with difficult to describe subtleties and concepts? It's easy enough to sell this product or that. You can show a picture of a pair of shoes, or a delicious meal, or a stylish piece of furniture, but how does one truly communicate the worth of a book? Even a masterful film can be advertised, however inadequately, through a two-minute preview. But write 200 pages of glorious text, and most of your opportunities to sell it will come from a clever title, subtitle, and cover image. It is an achievement just to get the back cover read, much less the text inside. The creation is difficult to sell, and the creator has difficulty selling—the enterprise is structurally inclined to fail.

Conclusion

It's not impossible to succeed as a writer, but there is a reason for the reflexive eye roll that comes over people when hearing of a writer's aspirations. Selling our writing is hard. It's even harder since, by virtue of our career choice, we're not very likely to enjoy the social demands of promotion. If any have a facility with language matched by a love of social interaction, better they become a politician and spare themselves the pains of editing. For all the rest of us, who found ourselves alone before a blank page by necessity, achieving success will be a difficult climb.

Still, the only insuperable obstacle is the one unrecognized. If, like me, you see clearly the fears to be faced and the ordeal to be endured, then I pray you understand that the only true barrier is ourselves, that one hand pushes against the other. If we were to find ourselves wrapped in yard after yard of chains, it might require only a tiny key to turn the lock and free us; in just the same way, it takes only a sliver of courage to unravel a lifetime of fear.

V

How to Deal With Being a Broke Writer

The want of money is usually the want of something else—something we should already possess

It is a common cliché that writers make little money. With few exceptions, the stereotype seems to bear out in reality. I have elsewhere written about some of the reasons why that is, but the why doesn't satisfy the lingering discontent. I wanted to address the disappointment experienced by writers directly.

Wealth

For all that our financial status informs our conception of the world and of ourselves, there are only three levels on which wealth has any value. The first is for subsistence. The rapper Kanye West once wrote that "having money isn't everything, not having it is."[1] Not having the money to fulfill basic wants and needs makes for a desperate and highly stressful situation. The want of money reaches its chief justification in these circumstances.

Next, we have money for pleasure. There are many who talk down on those who are materialistic, but none who disregard beauty and joy. Yet, money can bring before you sights to marvel the eye, scents and tastes that warm the soul, and the finest and gentlest of fabrics and climes. It can arrange a trip for you this very minute so that you might witness the grandeur of the Norwegian fjord, the jungles of Brazil, or the aurora borealis dancing in the Arctic sky. Perhaps, I wish to live a simple life of comfort in a home by the river. Where in that is the want of money? Yet, the dream remains unattainable without enough capital to furnish what would be needed year after year. The sparkle of a diamond, the sunrise on the shore, the mountain top above the clouds—all of these are fragments of God, but it is a dirty piece of cloth that grants one continued, ready access to them. Money is only a means to worldly things, but so much of the world is a means to something higher.

The third reason we want money is for status, but even this is not as superficial as it sounds. We want to appear accomplished, capable, and as if we have our lives neatly pieced together. Having wealth paints that picture nicely. The tragedy of worrying about how we're perceived by others is that we're never quite able to get a clear understanding of how it is they truly see us. Ultimately, our conception of how others perceive us is just a reflection of how we see ourselves. We work to hide our insecurities from them, as if they were as glaringly obvious to them as they are to us. In truth, most people think more of us than we imagine—and think *about us* far less than we imagine. Still, the human condition is rife with angst, and we are pestered constantly with doubts about our personal value. This hunt for status becomes but the gathering of evidence in support of a single statement: "I am worthy."

The primary reason we want money is to seem worthy, in our eyes and the eyes of others. We wish to feel accomplished, as if we have actually done something so significant that it is deserving of this grand recompense. Somewhere deep down inside, every impoverished person asks themselves, *If I am not worthless, why am I not worth more?* Where is my reward, and if it has yet to arrive, and may never arrive, is it because I am not deserving of it? That haunting question drives so much of why we come to crave wealth.

I will add here an aside about generosity: To provide all of these things for others, as the gifts of our love, might be considered another potential motivation, but it is simply an extension of these three reasons. It is not a different motivation but a context for the same motivations, one wherein we still wish for these three things, but so that we might also confer them on others.

To live, to live well, and to live with a sense of pride, for these reasons we crave wealth. On the topic of subsistence, there is no argument to be made: For this, money is required. As to the second reason, to please the senses, money certainly simplifies the pursuit. It is a hard road to many of the world's treasures without riches to pave the way. It is only the last reason for pursuing wealth—to demonstrate one's personal value—that I take exception with.

Work

You have worked so hard at your craft, but you have yet to be rewarded. Neither fame, nor wealth, nor acknowledgment come to you. At the cost of enormous effort, you have brought forth grand and complex projects, but they go almost completely overlooked by all around you. It begs the question: What is merit?

A friend of mine, an accomplished lawyer, one time asked what I had been working on that month, and I showed them. They were taken aback with surprise, and said, "You work harder than I do!" Unbeknownst to them, I had been putting an equal amount of effort into another undertaking, which I didn't yet want to disclose. At that time, I had received pennies for my writing, while they made hundreds of thousands of dollars every year. A few months later, we got into an argument, and I had earlier that day complained about financial difficulties, so they told me, "If you need money, you should get a job, like everyone else," as if I were without because I was lazy and unwilling to work. Everyone seems to espouse the belief that hard work is what makes a person, but hard work without reward—hard work that results in nothing more than failure and destitution—is, in truth, rarely considered any more laudable than failure and destitution due to apathy. Society doesn't celebrate effort, only outcomes.

Recently, I sat down with someone close to me to watch an interview given by their employer. He began talking about how hard he had worked to build the company. "I spent 6 months in the basement, working like crazy," he said, among other things, "I didn't even think about getting a girlfriend or anything." After it ended, my familiar turned to me full of enthusiasm and went on about how inspired they were. I was left confused: We see *real* hard work all around us, so why are we only moved when we hear this fluff about hard work from someone wealthy? It's because we're being sold a dream.

The son of some businessman, upon becoming an adult, receives access to his father's network and a few million dollars. He needn't have a skill to speak of. He wishes to create a company with a business model no different from a thousand others, so he pays people to perform each role within it—and a recruiter to find them. Left to their own devices, those talented individuals create value; they can even tolerate some degree of mismanagement; and would thrive under any company head with basic competence. The business booms. The fortunate scion's name is on the records as chief executive, so he is soon a success in his own right. Now, alongside of every other advantage, there is the addition of social proof, in the form of a track record of achievement. It can then be said that he is excellent at making deals and bringing in clients. Who doesn't want to partner with a team with proven results?

When he speaks on his success, he, of course, attributes it to hard work. The listeners are inspired. They take to heart that hard work can earn you the lavish parties, the trips to incredible destinations, and all the glamour of that world, and at such a young age to boot. To be fair, the wealthy executive has likely worked relatively hard. No doubt he has spent late nights discussing projects and even takes business calls while on vacation. Meanwhile, I have a childhood friend who currently works two jobs, because of this he often ends up working a 12-hour shift through the night at a warehouse, and in the morning, with no time to sleep in between, does a 9-hour shift doing construction. He also has aspirations of being an Olympic runner, so he trains in his time off. He has no car and lives with his parents, despite being in his late twenties. The inheritor is acknowledged as a success by all, and my friend is constantly being deemed a loser. If wealth is the measure of merit, then hard work does not make one meritorious.

Is it talent, then, that we look at as the necessary prerequisite for riches? Does the money signify our competence? I'd ask the reader to rely on their own experiences and to search their memory banks for how often they've seen, or have themselves been, a competent underling working for an inept higher-up. Everywhere you look there are fools at the highest levels. Many of the most powerful people are incredibly competent but many more are not. If only truly competent people were in power, the world would be unrecognizable. List the most serious problems faced by our species, and you will find that they are all man-made. There is no shortage of genius; it is simply kept to the fringes. I could bore the reader with a list of physicists, philosophers, inventors, poets, etc., of the highest strain of genius, who lived and died in poverty.

Worth

You believe you must become wealthy if it is deserved, but when has wealth ever gone where it is deserved? You believe you must be unworthy if you have not been duly compensated. It is a sign of one's goodness, as well as a heartbreaking naivety, to believe deep down in such a fair society as to deem oneself unworthy for being without reward. Stand as your own judge. Have the hours drifted by like countless grains of sand as you've labored after your dream? Have you worked at this and that, stopped and started, failed and tried again in pursuit of those visions that you fantasize about so obsessively? Has your level of skill, no matter how far from perfection, improved many times over from where you started? I say you are worthy, and lest you prove the world right by here acting the part of the fool, I suggest you acknowledge that fact as well. Merit is hard work. Merit is talent. The world has said otherwise. The world has said possession of its rewards is an indicator of merit, and the world is wrong.

All you hope to obtain has been handed to senseless babes at the moment of their birth, and many of them grew into senseless adults, believing that they are deserving of all they enjoy. Meanwhile, entire populations have lived life restricted by sundry disadvantages, and they have been looked on by others as undeserving—and have even looked on themselves as such. Society can keep us from what we deserve, and it takes a particular sort of cunning to remedy this discrepancy. However, the true battle to be fought is in the seat of the soul, wherein you must take an accounting of your life and proclaim to yourself and all others that you are undoubtedly worthy.

VI

Why the People Closest to You Might Not Love Your Writing

Having a personal relationship with someone can keep them from seeing your work for what it is

A writer's confidence is a wobbly thing. What seemed to be a masterful piece of writing this morning often becomes a worthless mound of words by nightfall, only to be profound again the next day. It is a punishment fit for Greek mythology: to be able to instantly and unequivocally assess the worth of every other writer's work, except one's own. We are too close to see the worth of our own writing clearly. In one mood, it looks to be skillful and beautiful; in another, it seems mundane and clunky.

Often, we look to those around us for reassurance. The role the people close to us play as emotional support can't be overstated. Sometimes we show them our work just because we so desperately want them to be proud of us; other times, we're forced to show them just because it's expected that what we have shared with the world we will also share with close relations. But the people who we most hope will enjoy and be supportive of our writing are often those who, for a number of reasons, find it the most difficult to be enthusiastic about our work.

The wrong book

I published my first book last year. My family and friends were all supportive; they each congratulated me and purchased themselves a copy. However, this led to a little mix-up recently. For holidays, if a person at all enjoys reading, I tend to get them books. Last year I read the book *Thoughts Are Things* by Prentice Mulford. Growing up my dad would always say "thoughts are things," and the ideas expressed in the book were very similar to his own. I wondered if it had been some formative piece of text for him that he had forgotten he read when he was younger. I got him a copy for Christmas. But, by the time I next saw him, it slipped my mind that I had given it to him.

At some point in our conversation that day, he turned to me and said, his eyes wide with excitement, "I forgot to tell you: It's a really great book. It's really something." I was touched. I could tell he really meant it. The thing is that for a couple of seconds I thought he was talking about the book I had written. Then, the carpet of happy misunderstanding was pulled from underneath me, and I remembered he was talking about Mulford's book. Imagine being saddened by someone saying "thank you" for a Christmas present. That, to me, exemplifies the sensitivity of writers. You put yourself out there in a way not many do, and while everyone else thinks of it in passing, for you it is all-consuming.

If a stranger, after purchasing the book leaves a review that is more critical than complimentary, they are simply expressing their opinion. But when I read that comment, I recall all the years of effort; the painstaking process of writing and rewriting, editing and editing more, which continues to this day and will likely never end; all of the thousands of dollars and hours of my time spent marketing; and all of that to ultimately be told that it wasn't very good. Well, if this was the best I could do, and it wasn't very good, then what am I?

It's thoughts like these, and the general sensitivity that accompanies the vulnerability of making one's writing public, that makes the emotional support of friends and family so important. But like so much when it comes to relationships, what we feel we need is more than we could ever even hope of giving another, if we were in a similar position, and therefore more than we could ever expect to get in return.

Too close

I have a good friend who makes music; specifically, he's a rapper. When I hear his music, there's something in it that stands out like a sore thumb and keeps me from appreciating it for what it is: his voice. It's not that his voice is bad or odd-sounding; it's just all too familiar. I try to listen to the song, but all I hear is Travis. When he raps some clever and boastful bar about his conquests with women or his wealth, I don't see the image he's painting; I see his actual girlfriend and his actual house. I know about the makeshift studio this was recorded in and his day job as a plumber. None of that detracts from the actual quality of the music, nor should it, but for me it's distracting.

Him playing the music for me makes it even more difficult to appreciate it for what it is. When we're in my car and he plays a new song, I can hardly sit back and enjoy the witty lines and catchy beat; I'm sitting there thinking about how to react. I'm thinking about what I can say I liked and how to come across as genuine in my appreciation for it. I can barely hear the actual music!

Moreover, there's a certain intimacy to complementing someone else's work, which can be uncomfortable if you're not used to it. If someone isn't the type to effusively say how much they care for you or otherwise make themselves vulnerable—even though they may love you to the ends of the Earth—it can be difficult to say how much they care for your work. Their emotional restraints don't disappear just because they want to be a good friend and supporter. There're no doubt a great number of times in their life when they wanted to be expressive and open up about their feelings but were unable to. Other times, people can't express their appreciation because it makes too clear in contrast their own failings. A family member who always wanted to write a book but never did might find themselves choked up by regret or even envy.

Whatever the reason, when we have a preexisting relationship with a person, everything that is attached to that goes into their response to our work. It could be a masterpiece, but the complicated personal factors at play can keep the people around us from being able to fully recognize or speak on its value.

The rapper Drake mentions in his song, "How Bout Now," how he once played his music for someone close to him and they quickly asked if they could listen to the rapper Ludacris's music instead.[1] There are people who would stampede over one another to hear Drake's music before anyone else, but the person he played it to probably just heard Aubrey Graham (Drake's real name). I've wanted to be a philosopher for the entirety of my adult life, but when my friends and family read my lofty words about principles and love, they probably just hear Martin. Martin who has made a million mistakes, embarrassed himself a thousand times, and slowly developed any skill as a writer by a slow and painful process of trial and error, which they've witnessed every step of.

The writers I see as geniuses were probably, for a time, seen as those around them as just some person trying to sound smart or dramatic. After the rest of the world recognizes us, those closest to us will likely follow suit, because they'll be able to see us through the eyes of others. But until that time, they'll never really be able to see our work; they'll just see plain ol' us.

Disconnect

Every writer has the voice they write in and the informal tone they speak to their familiars with. I doubt Oscar Wilde found occasion for such dramatic lines as "We're all in the gutter, but some of us are looking at the stars," when discussing what to have for lunch each day.[2] From afar, when we only know a writer by their works, we can let them be 100% who they are as a writer; it doesn't come across as someone writing in an affected way, completely different from the way they usually speak. We know only their writing voice, and so however dramatic or profound their words are, it's able to assume a complete naturalness.

We can take Nietzsche completely serious when he writes, "I say unto you: one must still have chaos in oneself to be able to give birth to a dancing star."[3] But his friends and family might've just rolled their eyes and said, "There goes Nietzsche, putting on his writing voice and trying to sound all grand and wise again."

To have one voice to write in and one voice to speak in is a natural part of being a writer. Surely not even Shakespeare ordered food in verse or felt the need to rhyme whenever he asked a member of his household if they had seen his doublet lying around somewhere. To witness his transition from one voice to the other would've been slightly jarring for some of the people in his life and given his writing an air of inauthenticity. But that didn't make Shakespeare any less of a truly talented writer.

Conclusion

There are lots of reasons why the people we know best, and whose opinions we value most, might not be able to give us the validation we crave as writers. It can be hard for the head to prevail over the wants of the heart, but we should do our best not to take it personally when the people close to us don't get excited about the writing we produce. Easier said than done—trust me, I know. But to be a writer means following our internal compass even when no one else believes in us. Getting someone to pay for our words, when they can readily make their own, or buy the words of any number of famous, brilliant people, was an audacious dream from the start. Don't lose that audacity just because the people around you can't see you for the writer you are.

VII

Should a Writer Be a Person or a Brand?

Career success comes from consistency, but this restricts creative freedom

Many people view an author as a brand. Readers expect a thematic consistency throughout a writer's works. It is an expectation that is applied by consumers to all creators. It is a natural occurrence: When we have thoroughly enjoyed one work, and we return to the source, looking for more of what we have so far liked, we hope for something of the same kind. Thus, when the musician who has typically made rock makes a foray into dance music, or the actor known for comedies tries their hand at drama, we are sometimes put off by the transition and prone to disappointment. The creative is caged by these expectations.

It is easy to see how there is commercial value in monotony. It allows us to establish a brand, and people will then come to us looking for that particular thing we do so well. It is simple and salable. For this reason, I have often been wary of touching on subjects that are too remote from one another. Still, I have written about love, design, morals, finance, physics, personal experiences, etc. It is a battle of the natural inspirations of artistry and curiosity versus the demands of commercialism, which pulls us towards one path or the other.

Creativity vs. consistency

There is a phasic periodicity to many a creative's natural inclinations. It can be found in short cycles, so that an article here and an article there touch on wildly divergent subjects, or it can be longer term, with a year dedicated to this and a year dedicated to that. The author might become something of a summer home, and readers will only show interest in their work for a season. All of this is just a reflection of life. If the rotation and evolution of our interests take us to a variety of places, if we have a beckoning curiosity or undertake a project that pulls us in a new direction every six months, how are we to stymie ourselves for the sake of our readers? What is the balance to be struck between consistency for the sake of a brand and inconsistency for the sake of freedom and natural development?

To enjoy great success as a writer, it seems to be logical, as well as anecdotally evidenced, that consistency is key. When we look at the works of the greats, we find that they rarely ventured outside the purview of their mastery, and when they did, the outcome was relatively subpar. Tolstoy and Emerson are both incredible, but I have found Tolstoy's non-fiction uninspired and would rather be spared Emerson's poetry. Selfishly, if given the option, I would've compelled each of them to stay within the arena of their primary competence: novels and essays, respectively. However, this relegates the author to only a portion of their whole. One can work as an author, but they are not an author: They are a human. They cannot be treated like a tree or bush in the garden, having all its branches clipped as soon as they move outside the bounds of some neat symmetry.

A whole person

As consumers, we must guard against our bias for sameness, and allow a writer to be something more than their writings. A work is only a work. I have read everything by Nietzsche I could find, but I have not read Nietzsche the man. I have no idea how he acted when he felt threatened, how he treated his friends and family, or how petulant he might've been when out of sorts. Frankly, I don't care to. There is a curiosity about the author that naturally follows any appreciation of their work, but we cannot fool ourselves into believing we are *actually* interested in the person behind the page.

In general, we tend to tie creatives to their work in an unusual way. It is startling when, for example, a musician capable of creating beautiful songs is found to have committed some despicable act. Often, people rebel at the thought that an R. Kelly or Steven Tyler could have done something deeply immoral because their productions are sublime. It seems incongruous because we have conferred on the creator some of the laudableness belonging to their creations. This is yet another way that we dehumanize the creative by reducing them to their works. Talent is only a single aspect of personhood. While what they make might be entirely good, the person behind it is bound to fall short of the mark in countless particulars.

A masterpiece can approach perfection, but a person never can. There is no homogeneity to the human spirit; it is all-inclusive. It encapsulates animal wants and volatile emotions, skewed perspectives and partial awareness, sharp reasoning and warm intentions, all into a single person. The soul is a messy place, and it is far too large to be perfect. You may hike through a jungle and find a flawless piece of fruit hanging from a tree. This fruit is akin to Dostoyevsky's *Crime and Punishment* or Mary Shelley's *Frankenstein*. A person is not so small as this, they are the tree—or the jungle itself. You will find all sorts of stunted productions and predators lurking within them.

On Authorship

Martin Luther King Jr. spoke to the whole world of its most important truths, and in a voice and literary style that raised up any who heard his words, but he could still turn and tell his wife a cold lie. Thomas Jefferson helped gift humanity the framework and organization for upholding the most consequential of values: freedom. This gift was promoted by many of the words that he spoke in his life, while many of the other words he spoke were no doubt commands given to his slaves. The cruelty of nature is in its haphazardness and unconsciousness. It is a miracle that humans came to exist, but they were not built by design. We are, each of us, a messy jumble.

We would have our creatives stop being human and exist only as their occupation. Anyone who has ever truly appreciated my work would have me give them something new but only as the species gives something new. Out in nature, every type of animal reproduces and each year there are new lemurs and elephants and kangaroos, each one with their own personality and look, but they are each far more similar to their conspecifics than they are different. The true spirit of the creative wishes to create as all of nature does: a star one day and a blossom the next, the sparkling diamond first and the lion cub to follow. The rainbow and the river are not in competition; there is no better or worse. Each has equal and superlative value. Every aspect of existence has the qualities of infinity, of the immeasurable: Each has no particular value, yet each has all value. I see beauty and wisdom in discussions about the stock market and sales techniques, just as I do in conversations about love and virtue.

Creatives

As writers, we struggle to have our work appreciated, but even when we have found our supporters, we must face the limitations they naturally place on us. How are we to contend with this? For some, this is of no concern; for others, it is unendurable. Everything in art—as with everything else in life—comes back to its source. In the case of art, the source is the motivation. If we create because we have no other choice, because something bubbles up deep inside and it will make its way to the surface no matter what, then perhaps we have an answer. We must facilitate its release, perfect its mode of expression, and perhaps we can create something worthy of being experienced by others, and we can be contented by that alone. If, however, we wish to draw a crowd, or fill our pockets, then we must make a factory of ourselves. The operation cannot pivot on a whim from one type of production to another. It must have a brand and a process. The world needs writers of every kind. Some speak to the needs of the soul and others to the demands of pragmatism; some seek to rouse and inspire, while others simply pass along information; some write on what will be irrelevant tomorrow, and others offer insights that will apply with unchanging exactitude in whatever millennium the work is encountered. In our lives, commercialism has its asks and so does curiosity.

Truthfully, the question of whether not a writer should or should not make a brand of themselves does not benefit from an answer. We can weigh the two options and plot our course, but the answer was housed in our bosom before we ever sought to look for it. Motivation precedes us. We do what we will each day before we ever stop to ask why, and even if we should try to do something else, the elasticity of our volition will exhaust itself, and we will be drawn back to whatever breath of life has galvanized us since the beginning. Today I decide I will write only on the one subject that interests me most, or brings to me the most faithful readers, but tomorrow I will not be able to muster any enthusiasm for this topic. Conversely, if I have come here to build a career, business, and brand, I will never be able to quiet my desire to write what is most salable. We are a ghost in our bodies; we watch while it moves. The pen goes where it will, and I follow, with either disappointment or satisfaction.

VIII

Is It Egotistical to Post Your Writings?

An exploration of the role of ego and narcissism in writing

Writers suffer from an odd sense of shame. Many couch their efforts behind a subtle disclaimer by calling themselves "aspiring writers," as if they're not writers until they're bestsellers, signed to a publishing deal, or featured in the *New York Times*—as if they were not writers since the very first day, likely as a child, when they decided to take pen to paper and spill some of their soul into the ink. Of course, some of this self-doubt comes from a fear of making claims beyond one's level of skill. However, as I've considered this topic, I've found another reason for it, one that lies at the core of the art of writing.

We believe we have to earn the title of writer because to write feels egotistical, and in some ways, it is. To write, and make our writings public, implies that what we have to say is so important it deserves to be recorded, and others should give up their valuable time to read it. But I wanted to undertake a deeper exploration of the role of ego and narcissism in writing. What I found is that, yes, writing involves a lot of what seems to be self-centeredness, but masterful writing is actually among the most humble practices a person can engage in.

Ego

We label anyone who monopolizes conversation an egotist, so why not those who forego the second party altogether and simply write out their thoughts? Writing is always a monologue. Even if it's structured in a story, behind all the characters and scenes it's just a person talking to themselves.

The act of making it public is only further evidence of narcissism. Imagine an individual has a thought one morning and begins typing about it on their computer. They take that first draft and slave over it for hours across the coming days—reworking it and editing it, again and again. Finally, they submit it for publication, or post it to a blog, because it's so important that all this time and effort had to be expended just so that the world might set their lucky eyes on it.

Moreover, there's little room for equivocation and reserve when practicing this craft. If we're going to type up a few thousand words and expect people to read them, we'd better have something to say and say it like we mean it. If the essence of writing wasn't inherently vain, the demands of good writing would seem to make it so.

To be a professional writer adds yet another point of audacity to the whole practice. Not only does one spend their time alone soliloquizing; then, think their words such a prize that others should fritter away their day consuming them; but, at last, they insist people pay for the privilege as well! It has all the hallmarks of a peculiar species of psychosis: Let us call it "authorial personality disorder." Mustn't we consider ourselves terribly self-important to try and take pen to paper for a living? I would contend that, despite all of this, the answer is a resounding "no."

Egoless

People have come up with all sorts of different explanations for what it means to be alive, but what really makes life what it is is expression. Doesn't a vine communicate quite clearly its want of light by twisting and climbing towards the sun? If it was egotistical to express, the skittish fish, the eager puppy, and the territorial bird, as well as every other living thing, would be tainted along with us.

A writer is, in fact, much more humble than all that. The true art of writing is egoless. There's only one type of truly bad writing, and the entire development of a writer's skill is found in defeating the cause of it: vanity. Bad writing is affected writing. When we try to sound a certain way—any type of way—we fail. The adage "write to express, not impress" is absolute. If one aims to be a great writer, they best stop aiming.

Good writing is self-acceptance. When we can say what it is we have to say, without dressing it up by trying to sound smart or stylish, it never fails to resonate. What fabric can be put on the body that is more magnificent than our skin? Good writing is a naked thing; it has no covers or adornments. To become a skilled writer is to do away with one's ego, and let what wants to flow flow, without interference or addition.

Bad writing is simply a sign that the writer *tried* to write. If we try to force this skill, we stunt it. To write well is to step aside. Where does inspiration come from? No one knows. It is hidden somewhere deep in our constitution. If a writer formulates their words intentionally, they do so only occasionally. For the most part, words pop into one's mind, and the writer simply transfers them onto a page. They are not the hand that writes or the brain that creates the words; they are fortunate observers, watching something larger than themselves working through them.

The universe, and its processes of rising complexity, specifically evolution, have created a being capable of representing concepts through symbols known as "words." There is a part of our brain that furnishes us with this ability. It does what it does, and we can supply it with fodder and exercise, but it is not us. We would never be able to hold a conversation if we had to consciously select each word from the thousands available; they simply flow forth from this incredible organ. We would surely be put off by any who thought themselves so important as to take credit for the workings of a lump of fat tucked away in their skull.

A writer is only half-awake. We admire this author or that for their genius and originality, but look to each supposed fountainhead and you will find that they are still only a derivative of a larger body—each fountainhead is only a rivulet flowing from the godhead. Like the river, the elements flow to us before they can flow from us, so that they only ever really flowed through, with no clear divisions between one portion and the other. The molecules in my body have formed a portion of a million different bodies before me: The minerals were once in stone, the protein once in other animals, and the water rained down from some divine cloudscape. Just because this body has been given my name, doesn't mean it truly belongs to me, and the same can be said for this piece of writing.

Language is a tool and a function. The writer is not an egotist for using their tool, any more than a digger is for swinging about their shovel. The writer is not an egotist for functioning as designed, any more than a bird is for flapping its wings. Life is expression. If this expression is of the deepest kind, of the soul expressing itself directly and in an unmistakable manner, as is the case for any true writer, then it is to be celebrated.

Even the humble aren't required to forego their guards. In Medieval France, adulterers were forced to walk naked through crowded streets with trumpeters in front of them to draw attention.[1] Good writing is something similar. What lengths I've gone to in order to get a few more eyes on a story about my most trying times! On a spectrum from prideful to shameless, writing certainly draws closer to the latter pole.

The best writing is self-sacrifice. One gives themselves up with such vulnerability that to do so they must pour salt in their wounds and bare their scars. If it didn't have the power to resonate with the reader, it would be an embarrassment, a source of humiliation. If it didn't disrobe the reader and make them feel naked right alongside us, it'd surely be met with derision.

Conclusion

There is no doubt that vanity leaves its mark on a lot of what's written. The haughty writer, in their black turtleneck, looking down on others through their glasses is the devil sitting on our shoulder; it certainly has its range of influence. On the other shoulder, however, is a godly force that passes through us and renders us little more than an instrument: namely, a vessel for experiences and a vehicle for the spirit. It's not egotistical to post your writings—if you're doing it right.

IX

Why Your Writing Might Be Too Good to Be Popular

It takes some degree of skill to recognize skill

I've often found myself stumped as to why certain things become popular while others don't, especially when a lot of the productions that seem to be of the highest quality end up relegated to a position on the fringe. Every day I come across stunningly beautiful songs, and they don't make it anywhere near the top 100, while the upper echelons seem forever occupied by the uninspired pop music of the day. I've gone to bookstores to find the philosophy section reduced to a few shelves, while the celebrity biographies and cliché self-help books span halfway across the store. At the movie theaters, it's the norm to find a veritable masterpiece of cinema being outperformed by 2 hours of videotaped explosions with the occasional interjection of dialogue. Why is it that what's most popular rarely seems to be the most deserving?

Our initial assumption is the most obvious: There's no accounting for taste. There's no way anyone can say what's better than something else. However, that's not entirely true. While we cannot say one production is "better," we can certainly make a nuanced argument about skill. I don't think I'd find anyone who would argue that the relatively obscure Coen Brother's film, *A Serious Man*, wasn't better written, acted, and directed than Zack Snyder's recent box-office juggernaut, the *Justice League* movie. Sure, it's apples to oranges, but plot holes are plot holes, cliché dialogue and tropes are demonstrably cliché, and bad acting is painfully obvious.

If we can replace the word "better," instead rephrasing it as "products that took a higher level of skill to create," we can pose the question more clearly: Why is it the pieces that require a more skilled hand to create—the masterpieces, if you will—are so often underappreciated? It takes skill to recognize skill.

The highest quality productions are inaccessible. They require technical understanding to appreciate. The lay person, which most consumers are, is only able to appreciate productions that are of a minimal complexity beyond their current understanding of any skill set. The highest quality wine, verse, music, and the like, will always be received best by a small, niche audience. It takes years to learn all the various intricacies that inform a skill before you can use it to create a masterpiece. Similarly, it takes years to really be able to appreciate those intricacies as a consumer.

The masterpiece is called as such because it is purposeful and virtuosic down into its finest details. It requires technical understanding and a significant depth of awareness to appreciate those subtle details that make a masterpiece a masterpiece. Conversely, a product that is relatively good, while still being readily accessible, will always make for a better market opportunity than one that is the best available but inaccessible. Popularity is a measure of how attractive a thing is, yes, but it is also a measure of how accessible, or obvious, those attractive qualities are.

It's a matter of time and effort. It's a lot easier to read through a self-help book whose only real innovative element is a brightly colored cover and a curse word in the title than it is to work through the complicated subtleties of Herman Hesse's *Siddhartha*. I could watch a superhero movie with neither sound nor subtitles and enjoy it purely for the exciting imagery, while the brilliant subtext in the horror/thriller *It Follows* needs to be thoughtfully considered in order to grasp it. A masterful creation is nuanced, and, by its nature, it takes time and effort to recognize nuance.

One considers themselves a sophisticate for having mastered some vaunted skill, but if we drop them in the thousand particular scenes that make up society, they will find themselves incompetent in all but a few. Life is not sufficiently long, nor is the human mind sufficiently powerful, to allow for anyone to have a knowledge of all things, or even half—or any more than a tiny fraction. A person with a great estate, complete with manor and enveloping forest and rivers, finds that it is smaller than a speck when looking upon the globe as a whole; a genius, though their mind contains countless particular facts and insights, holds less than a drop of the ocean of obtainable knowledge. Look to the writings of the most prolific author, and you will find that Shakespeare, or Aristotle, or any other, occupies a single shelf in the endless maze that is the complete library of humanity's works. It is no wonder that the expertise in many fields will be wasted, for only those rare few who have chosen to walk that single path in pursuit of their predecessors, in the place of any one of the infinite other walks of life, will find the treasures there concealed.

It is disheartening that society as a whole is seldom able to recognize the most talented individuals in any field. Sometimes it makes for tragedies, such as allowing the likes of Edgar Allen Poe, Herman Melville, and Emily Dickinson to all die without their due deserts. Fortunately, while the battle for recognition is often harder for the truly meritorious, it is far from impossible. People love to cast derogations on the critics of food, film, music, literature, and the like, for getting too into the details. These sometimes overly technical individuals can seem detached, uppity, unable to appreciate things with levity, and predisposed to those of their own ilk—other snobby elites and intellectuals. However, they provide an invaluable service. These individuals with technical understanding, and the committees they form, can serve as the last refuge for all of those deserving works that don't get their due from the larger public, and they often do a great job at fulfilling that role. It's hardly a challenge to find a finely crafted film being outperformed by a cruder creation at the box office, but it's very difficult to find a truly excellent film that hasn't received some acknowledgment from one association of savants or another.

The idea that your work might be too good to be popular isn't sure to bring much relief to any starving artists. Moreover, it's likely to be a small minority that could bestow upon themselves that consoling distinction with any real accuracy. Yet, out there in the world, there are thousands, if not millions, of individuals who have poured themselves into their craft and deserve much more in return for their productions than they're currently receiving. To them, hopefully it serves as some small source of solace: Your work might be *too good* to be popular.

Popularity is the want of many, and a want of mine as well. Nonetheless, it's not my intention to imply it is a thing of true value. Popularity is as mean and material as anything else of the world. Indeed, the primary reason it is sought after is to be a bridge to other material benefits. We want popularity mostly as a means to money, other social rewards, or the gratification of the ego. To say a work is "too good to be popular" can be rightfully interpreted to have a much deeper meaning: The work has higher aims than popularity.

True talent is marked by a disregard for petty popularity. The very essence of artistry is to ignore any wants but one's own, express without restraint, and paint the clearest picture of the universal by putting forward the unadulterated individual. A masterpiece strikes at the heart because it arose from one; it is etched on the soul and brought forth by an inward eye. Their creators are a self-contained world, serving as author, audience, and critic all in one. The strictest standard is their own, and they are satisfied in full by having met it. Though all the world may turn a blind eye to them, they cannot themselves in earnest deny the value of their works.

Moreover, what we call "popularity" is in many ways a superficial conception of what true popularity is. Popularity, as we view it, is a measure of pace, not extent. I've invoked Poe, Dickinson, and Melville, and they are each household names now, centuries after they've passed. The length of time their celebrity has endured for makes it all the more significant. If popularity is recognition that rushes all at once, greatness is recognition that abides. These giants couldn't escape discovery on a long enough time frame any more than they were able to attain fame over the course of their lives. However tardy its arrival, recognition never fails to come to merit.

Short-lived popularity is a product of marketing, not mastery. To garner attention is a dubious achievement. Any shameless loudmouth can draw a crowd. It is a menagerie of lowly things that make for facile diversions, but while shouting and scandal can earn a momentary glance, only substance can keep the eye trained. Above the rabble's din there is the eternal silence of the mountain top.

Genius is sometimes to be pitied because genius is, by definition, a stranger to the commons, and therefore, genius is lonely. Great talents are only ever seen in full by other great talents. Still, the blades of grass are crowded round, but their time is short-lived. The stars are only found one to each expanse, but they are immortal. Let each shining soul put forward its work, and though it may be neglected in damp confines for the next hundred years, if another light of this world will set eyes on it once each century, it will have ample audience among the gods.

In the immortal words of Ralph Waldo Emerson, "Leave to the diamond its ages to grow, nor expect to accelerate the births of the eternal."[1]

X

Why Having the Courage to Be Authentic Is the Key to Success

Fundamentally, our individuality is the essence of our value, while courage and authenticity are the means to demonstrating and actualizing it

Confidence and courage allow us to be authentic. Authenticity allows us to be our unique selves. Individuality and uniqueness are the cornerstones of our mortal prowess. Each of these virtues acts as a door, which we must open and open entirely, to access and release the fundamental source of power native to each of us.

Genius is a niche

Nature has allotted to us all some measure of genius by way of our individuality. Any writer can look at the writings of another, and though that author may outperform them on nearly all counts, there will always be one thing that they do better. Kant could maintain a more consistent logical thread than Emerson; Emerson could form a clearer analogy than Nietzsche; Nietzsche could construct an aphorism better than Aristotle; Aristotle could analyze a subject matter more thoroughly than Nietzsche. And so it is that Melville writes prettier than Tolstoy, but Tolstoy can describe human psychology better than Melville. Dumas understood the dramatic elements of romanticism better than any other, but he couldn't create a paradox that was both enlightening and impossible like Wilde did so effortlessly. All genius is a niche.

This is the case for as many different forms as human occupation, skill, and interest can take. There are instances where height is an advantage and others where smallness is. It is sometimes to one's benefit to be outspoken; other times it is advantageous to be silent. The athlete underperforms in the classroom, and the intellectual underperforms on the track. To expand our single point of unique aptitude into a life's worth of development and expression is the key to genius. We must sprint hungrily towards our interests, however unusual they might seem to others. We must spend every day cultivating our passion, for it alone is the fertile soil wherein the seed of our dreams can grow into a reality.

Cornering the market

With uniqueness comes an inherent lowering of competition. The consumer cannot satisfy their need for furniture by the purchasing of produce, any more than one can satisfy their hunger by purchasing clothes. Within the grander market, there are circles within circles of competition, within which only a select few belong. The population of our competitors is decided by the degree of our similarity. To be truly unique is to be without competition.

The fledgling in either business or art, if rightly idiosyncratic in their approach, may lament the fact that they have no institutions or individuals to aid them in their development due to their singularity. Where does one find a school that teaches, in a single course of study, the rare hybrid of competencies that marks you as a person? What marketing agency or publication focuses on your distinctive area of proficiency?

One can be dissuaded from authenticity on the basis that what frees one from competitors also separates one from friends and forces them from pre-established paths.

Fortunately, there are two sides to commerce. And though one who puts forward an entirely original product finds themselves without any other to rely on, they shall also find, opposite this, a loyal group of consumers who are enthusiastic about creations never before encountered.

Authenticity is the best politics

A person with a cold and direct manner of communication, if it seems authentic, is more endearing than one who is trying to be kind and warm but fails to come across as genuine. There are many a lovable curmudgeon, but all of us are repulsed by sycophancy.

There can be no blame for being faithful to one's nature. No person has ever designed themselves. Our decisions in regards to our person are not qualitative. We have only one axis of movement by which we can determine ourselves: We are what we are and can only decide whether to be less or more so; as a faucet does not put forth variously air, fire, water, or soil by a turn of the handle, but only allows a single element to pour forth, either in a slow trickle or a frenetic rush, so too must each of us decide how torrential of an outpouring of the essence of our soul we will allow for; or if we would instead rust away as a closed spigot, which failed to perform the only function that it was ever allowed.

All that is in accordance with one's nature is forgiven, for the purview of volition begins not at the design of the soul, but at the faithful adherence to its predetermined wants. Before we are individuals, we are humans; before humans, we are alive; and before we are alive, we are extant. The shared unity of all things in existence cannot be mocked or shamed in earnest, for if we scorn another's true self, we scorn ourselves as well. To be is to be loved. None of us is hated by any other person, and we do not hate any other person; it is only the masks we wear that instinctively draw ire for standing impertinently in the place of the true face of the soul.

Authenticity means commonality

We're just as much alike as we are different. When we can be our true selves it resonates with others. We've all met someone who is so unconcerned with what other people think of them that it inspires us. We all want to be that person who dances wildly at the party or wears a glam outfit like it was the skin they were born in. We hide so much of what we all feel inside that being ourselves is, more than anything else, what everyone wants to be. There's nothing unique about wanting to be unique and authentic, even if your authentic self is completely individual and unrepeatable, it is an aim you share with all others. Though it entails diverging paths, to be genuine is a common goal; just as we would all soar to different places, but our desire to take to the skies is uniform throughout all people.

Greatness is rare

In any distribution, for there to be outliers, whether high above or far below the average, they must, by this very fact of divergence from the mean, be individual, rare, and eccentric. By definition, greatness is uncommon. It must necessarily be a consequence of uniqueness, of something that is particular about the individual. Fortunately, uniqueness is vouchsafed to each of us as a birthright. Bold authenticity is the means to releasing that uniqueness in its full glory. You simply cannot be great, if you cannot be unabashedly yourself.

Unoriginal

It is the wont of any good writer to worry about being original. We can all be reassured that there is such a vast range to existence, and such a detailed texture to the things that exist, that even between the most similar entities there is still an infinite gulf of distinction. You and I are from afar almost entirely identical, yet they could fill endless libraries with a thorough cataloguing of our differences. It is the universe within this sliver of dissimilitude that is ours to explore and profit from. We may exist as only a fraction of full originality, but we are wholly individual as a particular sum.

Truly, there is equal power in both parts. When we can bring forth what is in us that mirrors what is inside all our fellows, we are able to reveal the truth felt inside of them, but which they could not firmly enough grab hold of to put into words. When we give of what is ours alone, we open a door into a new world and become for our brothers and sisters a foreign land, capable of teaching and enticing with infinite new discoveries. Whether we are to guide others inward, deep into the caverns and depths of their own soul, or we are to act as moral astronomers, charting the unreachable stars of a life that can be seen though it will never be lived, we find in our very essence the map for both paths.

Conclusion

Our unique essence is the only true power available to any of us. It is the formless substance that can be made into genius, greatness, lovability, compatibility, salability, and every other conceivable advantage in life. Courage is a means to authenticity, which is in turn a means to actuating the fountain of individuality that is our primary potency. This dictate shouldn't be as difficult to follow as it is: Boldly do whatsoever you will.

XI

Why You Should Write Less

Many writers seem to misunderstand the nature of what they do, and this leads to them becoming horribly hurried and overworked

I read articles, time and time again, from successful writers attributing their career accomplishments to waking up at 6 A.M. every day and writing for some set period. There is, perhaps, some advantage to be had in constantly producing content; I suppose your readers may be able to rely more fully on you for advice or entertainment or whatever it is you're writing on. But this approach disregards the true power writing: A written work is everlasting.

I've often weighed whether I should aim to produce two good articles a week or take my time and put out one great article every two weeks. The results in terms of readership are clear; an overwhelming amount of my "reads" every week occur from those pieces that were of the highest quality and were accepted to top publications. Beyond this empirical evidence, one can logically reach the conclusion that, if the writing is to exist and potentially garner attention for all of time hereafter, it should never be rushed, and instead the priority should be on creating quality work.

Indeed, writers on certain subjects are not equally entitled to the infinitely enduring value a piece of writing can possess. If one writes on current affairs, for example, rushing may become a necessity. This may serve as incentive to focus on subjects less susceptible to obsolescence. At any rate, even accounts of current affairs age into historical accounts, so there can be an advantage to proceeding with patient assiduity.

You are what you eat

Any writer who starves themselves of great written works will in turn starve their readers of any great written works. Your skill in writing, the ease with which you can develop insights, and the elegance of your style are all gained through your literary diet. No matter what subject you write on, you must digest works of fiction, poetry, and particularly inspired pieces of non-fiction—and each of these only ever of the highest quality.

There is no sheep so gifted that it can transform subpar feed into the finest wool, and there is no writer so talented that they can, on a diet of reality television and tabloids, produce quality writing. There is far too much emphasis put on practice and far too little put on diet. Just as with the bodybuilders and athletes, diet and digestion are as critical to development as exercise.

Oh, sweet brevity

In what area of life do we not prefer to get more from doing less? So it is for the lazy reader in us all, who prefers always a mote-sized diamond to a mountain of gravel. Better a paragraph of the highest quality than a dissertation's worth of mediocre writing.

You are an inexhaustible well

It gives me such confidence and calm when writing to know that I'll always have something to say, for I'm drawing from a bottomless reservoir. The physical reality is infinite in both space and time, and even if you do not allow for this, it still must be functionally infinite for you, who occupies such a tiny pocket of the grander whole.

Any one happening in this interminable procession begets many times more particular aspects and relationships to be observed and treated of. Each of these particulars can be viewed in a million different lights, and any thoughts which they inspire can be worded in yet another million manners.

There will never come a day when the world has run dry of experiences to put before you, and so there will never be a day when the writer is bereft of fodder from which to produce words. For a second time and a second reason, don't rush: Inspiration is on its way to you and always will be.

XII

Why You Should Care Less About Your Writing

As writers, we tend to take our craft very, very seriously, so here are some reasons to relax

I, like you, care way too much about what I say in my writing. There isn't a writer alive who doesn't know the feeling of toying with a good piece of writing so much that, in hopes of making it better, you end up ruining it. To quell my anxiety, I wanted to delve into the question of whether I should care so much, and I found a lot of reasons why we should all care a little less.

The underappreciated first draft

It can be difficult to get things just right in a first draft, but there is an important aspect of our writing that is rarely ever improved upon by redrafting: the flow. When the words we write flow smoothly and involuntarily from us, they have a smooth flow to whomever reads them.

When we edit our work we do so in a piecemeal fashion. We add a sentence here, take out a word there, and rearrange clauses throughout. This is inherently disruptive of the flow. Writing is thinking on paper, and thinking occurs in a contiguous procession, one thought leading to another, like links in a chain. A first draft is the genuine article; it is the thought process transformed into inky symbols. The editing process is the addition, removal, or rearrangement of links in this original chain.

It's for this reason that toying with a work too much often takes it further from perfection. And we tend engage in this process of over-editing because of worry over the quality of the original draft. We should try and care a little less about whatever slight flaws we notice to better preserve the all-important feature of flow.

Forget about it

Children should not be neglected, but the best thing you can do for a piece of writing is forget that you wrote it. When we leave a piece of writing alone for a time—allowing ourselves to forget exactly what it says before setting eyes upon it again—we return to it not as a writer but as a reader. Every flaw that we were too close to see, because we were supplementing what we actually said with what we intended to say, will now be painfully obvious. As anyone who has ever been in love knows, it's impossible to forget about what you care deeply for, so, please, care a little less about what you write.

Diffidence and writing don't mix

There's no easier way to take away the power of a statement than by couching it with "I think" or "in my opinion." The blank document before us each morning is our kingdom, and we should treat it with a sense of ownership. As long as a name is on it, every reader is well aware to whom the opinions belong. Every line should be written as if it were an axiom.

Grammar doesn't matter

Just the other day I was reading an email sent from the writer of a popular blog and newsletter, and I noticed she used "backbone" as a verb. It was something along the lines of "the profound insight backbones the story." I thought to myself, "Humph, that's not even correct English." And yet, she has many, many more readers than I do.

To whom am I to complain of this perceived injustice? Where are the gods of grammar to rectify this obvious mistake in the karma of the literary universe? There are none. The only thing that matters is the readers and whether or not they're finding value in our writing.

Read your favorite classic, and I guarantee you'll find some dependent clause starting with a conjunction and preceded by an unnecessary comma. Just as I can guarantee you'll find some sentence fragment put as a stand alone sentence. The truth of the matter is, unless you're in English class, grammar doesn't matter. The only thing that matters is that your readers understand and enjoy your work. Grammar is only a tool to that end, and other than some syntactical elements, grammar doesn't matter much at all.

Breaking the rules

Broken rules are a casualty of signature style. In *Anna Karenina*, considered by some as the best novel of all time, Tolstoy gives only one chapter (of hundreds) a title. Bram Stoker's *Dracula* is written as a collection of letters. Ludwig Wittgenstein wrote *Tractatus Logico-Philosophicus* as a procession of standalone, numbered, declarative statements.

Style is always flirtation. It is a challenge to be bold but smooth, daring but subtle. One must break the rules but with tact; this is the balance to be struck. The rules are made for everyone to follow. If you don't want to be like everyone else, why would you take them so seriously?

Trash can

There are few ways to more easily improve one's writing than by reading great writing, but perhaps even more important than what a writer consumes is what they excrete. The only way to become a good writer is to throw out a lot of bad writing. The only thing more important than a trip to the library is a trip to the trash can.

Every piece of writing contains a fragment of a person's essence, because of this there is seldom a piece of writing that doesn't have some gem of wisdom or beauty in it. Often it just gets lost around a lot of other stuff that isn't as essential to the author. Sometimes we throw in redundant and unnecessary fluff to drive a point home, fix (real and imagined) problems with flow, or to simply meet a desired word count.

In cases like this, is it not a problem of caring too much, of attributing too much importance to the surrounding sentences, instead of pruning down the piece and letting the magnificent portions shine in their full splendor? We should care less about what's inessential, so we can care a little more about what we really want to say.

If you're like me, nearly every sentence has some particular significance to you. It takes a callous disregard for this sentimentality to discard unworthy and incompatible lines. Each of us loves the things we write, but regardless we can't be afraid to throw them away.

All promotion is shameless

As someone who has suffered from terrible social anxiety, I know well how difficult it is to self-promote. The term "shameless promotion" is redundant. All promotion should be shameless. But the truth is that underqualified and overly arrogant people are beating out skilled, hard-working people every single day because they're not afraid to promote themselves.

This can be particularly difficult with writing, which is so personal. One should always write for oneself, and never for views or money, but getting more people to see your writing—expanding on your ability to have your heartfelt messages reach people—is not in anyway something to be ashamed of.

Authenticity isn't selfish

It is an unfortunate irony that, as writers, we tend to write things that are completely unrelatable because we're trying so hard to be relatable. Each of us has a voice in our head telling us exactly what we want to say, but we ignore it because we think it won't resonate with others. What we fail to realize is that the voice in our head is exactly the same as the voice in everyone else's head. When we describe exactly how we feel, it will always resonate with others. It's only when we try to guess at what some imagined person wants to hear that we lose sight of what we're all actually experiencing.

Readers are the smartest people

We often fret over whether or not we'll be understood, or if we can use some advanced word or concept, but we forget that there is hardly a more accurate indicator of a person's intelligence than their propensity to enjoy reading. A writer must give their readers some credit and themselves some slack. Say all that you have to say without concern over whether or not you will be understood.

Skill is only a window

To the artist, skill is like a sheet of glass. Behind the glass is the artist's vision, what they see and feel, and with a tireless effort they improve their skill, and the glass becomes cleaner, clearer, and less opaque, so that the person viewing the art can see more and more clearly that vision. The vision, or the art itself, has always been inside of you since the beginning. It is of an incomparably high quality, indescribable in its complete perfection. We applaud skilled artists for being able to bring the art out of themselves, but every person has inside of them a masterpiece.

Skill takes time to develop, but the sentiments are there from the start. It might take time until you can say something beautifully, but you can say something beautiful right now. The essence of your writing has been with you from the beginning, will accompany you throughout, and will never leave you. From the time when we can barely string a sentence together to the time that we're master writers, the spirit of our writing remains unchanged.

Writing is a form of expression, but what's being expressed is you and your ideas. Maybe it'd come through a tad clearer if you'd joined those two independent clauses with a semi-colon instead of a comma, but we get the message nonetheless. Once more, rest easy, for you will be understood.

Anxiety stifles creativity

It's difficult to describe the state of mind wherein we are the most creative, particularly because it's so different from person to person, but it is certainly not an anxious state. The state of optimal creativity feels like openness; it is an intellectual and emotional outpowering. It feels like any other release. And the distracted, frenzied, and withdrawn feeling of anxiety is about as close to the opposite of this as one can get. If we put too much significance into what we're writing, and as a consequence fret over every microscopic detail, we're sure to produce subpar work.

A writer's fears

As writers, the things we fear are far removed from the reasons we write. We all started writing because we love the craft. We want to express ourselves, and we want to get better at doing so. The fear is that we will make a fool of ourselves by saying something stupid or controversial, or demonstrate our ineptitude when it comes to style or technical form. Our first motivation was, and still should be, to express ourselves: to take a part of ourselves and our experience and gift it to the world. If you set out to, you will absolutely accomplish that. That's not related to skill or style or any of the other things we fear being judged on. Speak honestly, and you will be heard.

A sad fact

The truth is that no one is ever going to read your writing as patiently and with as much attention to detail as you wrote it with. Right now there is someone quickly skimming over this paragraph, barely keeping hold of the thread of thought. This doesn't excuse a writer from producing thoroughly developed writing, but it does allow us some solace in knowing that whatever imperfections we can't help but notice in our own writing are likely being completely missed by our readers.

Worst-case scenario

Shoddy work doesn't attract attention. If you write something excellent and make it public, you can be sure someone will take the time to share an unfavorable opinion with you. But if you write something second-rate, no one is going to criticize it: They're not going to read it all. It's a fortunate trade-off in writing.

The ghost of writing past

It's a wonderful feeling to write something you're truly proud of. However, it's scary to write something you're too proud of. There is a fear that it will be the last good thing you ever create. Like so many things in life, just by thinking of it it becomes a self-fulfilling prophecy. We are distracted by our past successes and by our desire to repeat them, and it suppresses our creative energy.

Conversely, every good writer instinctively hates what they wrote the year before. It's a natural consequence of development and optimism. For the future to look brighter, the past must be made a little darker. There is an Irish blessing that says, "May the saddest day of your future be no worse than the happiest day of your past."[1] Well, let's say instead, "May every piece you write in the future be no worse than the best piece you wrote in the past." And with that, whether it's because it was so good or so bad, let us a care little less about what we wrote yesterday, so that we can care more about what we'll write today.

Conclusion

There are a hundred different fears that spring up in the mind of a writer. The scale his heavily weighted in favor of caring too much. Let the reasons above serve as just a tiny bit of counterbalance.

Don't be careless, but care less.

XIII

Why Reading Is Essential for Writers

*The best way to become a better writer
is to become a better reader*

We have no words in us at birth. They were given to us by others, and over time we accumulated them. At this stage we may have such an abundant supply that we deem any further renewal from the source unnecessary. Don't be mistaken. The basin of words within each of us drains slowly, but it drains nonetheless. If we wish to spill forth each day onto the page, we must each day return to the well of another and drink from a cistern of linguistic genius.

Often, the fountain of our words runs dry, and we fret over and wonder at what has extinguished temporarily that creative spark. We have mistaken ourselves for the source. Writer's block should be a reader's bridge, taking us back to those majestic printed receptacles that contain all of the world's wisdom and knowledge.

A writer isn't actually one who is good at writing. This person we call a calligraphist. A writer's skill lies in thought and language. We practice language both as we use it and as we decipher another's usage of it, though only the latter can present to us the forms of mastery that are currently beyond our reach. Likewise, one gains capacity for thinking both from performing the act itself and from imbibing the thoughts of others. Any writer who both humbles us and riles us to envy with their matchless skill is not a better writer; they have simply had better feed. They have partaken of better books and more abundantly. The best writer is the best reader.

Quality

There is something worth reading in every book, just as one is able to get a full stomach from any restaurant. However, a world-class chef considers it their duty to consume and be influenced by only inventive and prodigious culinary constructions. The masterful musician by necessity rejects low-quality and uninspired songs. The discerning palate used in creation cannot be turned off for consumption. The writer should read with as a high a standard as they wish to write.

To read as a writer is to be immersed in genius and to allow, by the influx of another's words, some of the qualities of that master's style and form to be infused in one's own skill for language. A writer is by necessity a picky reader. If the book in our hands is to be absorbed into us, to become one of many rivulets of influence that by their confluence supply the wellspring of our ability, why would we ever set eyes on the words of the unremarkable and inflated authors of the day? The quality of the thought and literary style we allow to seed the fertile soil of the mind will determine the quality of its outgrowths. When an author chooses what to read, they also choose what to write.

No matter how shabby and stunted my own writing might be, any defect in it was not gained, but only ever improved upon, by my time spent with Emerson or Nietzsche, Shakespeare or Dickinson, Wilde or Dumas, Frost or Dante.

Dictionary

The bulk of the words we learn are not from the dictionary. We learned them, unintentionally, over years of reading and hearing them. For this reason, we tend to learn words inside of patterns. We use them in short phrases and idioms that are commonly passed around. Great authors learn a word in full. Instead of using "integrity" as everyone else does, to describe an aspect of moral character, they might use it to describe the quality of completeness, as Emerson does when he writes: "We mean the integrity of impression made by manifold natural objects."[1] Or when the word "attendant" is used not to describe one whose job it is to perform a service, but to describe something that follows or accompanies, as Robert Stone did when he wrote: "Civilization and its attendant morality are not structures, they're more like notions, and sometimes they can seem very distant notions."[2] And so it is that whenever we say "the meteor of snowfall outside the window" or "the zodiac of the rising and setting sun" we have taken something commonplace and shown a new side to it, and there's a subtle beauty in this.

One can sit and read the dictionary to learn new words, but this is like seeing an animal in a zoo; we may learn of its appearance, but until we have seen it in the wild, seen it acting out its life in full—with the ferocity of the hunt, the habits of migration or hibernation, the tenderness it shows its young, and the clashes with its conspecifics—we will not understand it. Words, too, were wild things before they were ever caged and classified. The first English dictionary was published in 1775,[3] whereas the English language had been spoken for a millennium prior.[4] In the dictionary, every part of speech is a noun, sitting there waiting to be utilized and acted upon; in literature, every part of speech is a verb, pregnant with the things of life, transporting them from one soul to another. We must witness words in a variety of contexts, observe them from every angle, and learn the full range of their function. One benefits from having a reference guide with them on their excursions into nature, but the animal on the page is not the animal in the wilderness.

Like a chemist, the writer, when reading, studies not only the macro things around them but the very elements that compose those things, so that one does not just see sentences and paragraphs, but gains an understanding of the atomic structure by investigating every conspicuous word down to its quiddity. I don't want to be misunderstood: The dictionary and the text itself are both invaluable. It is the interplay that is necessary. One encounters a word's less common usage through text and refines their vague notion of its new meaning by viewing it through the exacting lens of the lexicographer. Time spent with literature in one hand and a dictionary in the other makes it so, when at last one goes to write, the pen and page feel all the lighter.

Essence

All writing leads to a single place. Writing is only ever a vessel, lens, or vehicle. It can house, show, or transport, but it cannot make anew. Even when it alters and imagines, it shifts only in appearance, for the essence remains unchanged; the most fanciful fiction only resonates in so far as it remains on some level faithful to the laws of causality and the imprimatur of logic. The ideals that form the invisible center of human existence—of Truth, Beauty, and Goodness— are necessarily at the center of all writing as well. Wherever we are headed on the road of our writing, we are not delayed in getting there by the time we take reading the words of another. We all walk together, on infinite different paths, to a single, shared, and sublime destination.

One who can read like a genius can write like a genius, and one who can write like a genius can read like one. This dawned on me in a moment of sudden epiphany, and the circumstances of this example are infinitely self-reaffirming, for I was reading one of my favorite authors' words about one of their favorite authors. I was reading Emerson (whose name by necessity has come up so many times in this piece, as it should in any work about virtuosity in writing), and he wrote of Shakespeare's genius. The first quote he adduced to show Shakespeare's inimitable prowess was this:

The ornament of beauty is Suspect
A crow which flies in heaven's sweetest air.[5]

My first reaction was not one of awe at the beauty of the sentiment. I just wondered to myself what this meant; I was confused. It occurred to me, then, that Emerson was not only a better writer than I am currently, but he was a much better reader, and that, indeed, he was a better writer because a better reader.

Both these men had opened the vault of the firmament and made their way to unworldly heaven. They existed on a plane of understanding beyond the one I currently occupy. How can I ever hope to compose a work of genius, if I have not even put forward the effort to understand genius? I see the path before me; any of us can, by a quick trip to the bookstore, gain for remarkably little money a miraculous masterpiece to hold in our hands. We all have had genius set before us, yet we turn from it for the sake of ease.

How many sentences have I quickly skipped over in my life, unwilling to confront the recondite use of language, unwilling to do the work necessary to attain its profound meaning? I have been granted a route to that ineffable place I wish to reach, as have each of you. We need only read as the writers we wish to become.

Classics

If you cannot readily find your way to genius, then let the sifter of time be your guide. If a work has endured for a few centuries or more, we can be sure there is merit to it. When one picks from the classics, that is, the works of the dead, it is as hard not to land upon genius, as it is to fall from a boat and not land on water.

Let our readers partake, for now, of the words of the living, but a writer should nearly always be a scavenger, enjoying the remains of genius from bygone ages. Those pieces of literature that have been granted the highest accolade, that of being called "classics," are the surest evidence that though merit is not entitled to reward on any definite time frame, it is sure to have its day. Wade into those precious works that seemingly will shine for all of eternity, like diamonds in the sands of time.

Conclusion

Whether we're writing, reading, or even carefully speaking, we increase our ability for language—language independent of any other particular. Let us, then, exercise this faculty with not only the works of geniuses, but of their best works, of those creations that marked the summit of their existence. It is not a theoretical exercise. Whosoever spends an hour or two today reading the work of a master author will find their writing has improved in some small way tomorrow. Just as readily as we can go to the store and buy foods containing proteins with the potential to make our muscles grow, we can go to the bookstore and find a cornucopia of nutriment to develop our skill in writing with.

Genius is there for the taking.

XIV

How Writing Heals Trauma

*The blank page is such a simple thing, but it has helped
me heal in profound and surprising ways*

I've always been drawn to writing about the things that hurt me, but I had never before sat down and contemplated why exactly that is. What I've found is that writing allows you to express yourself in a place entirely in your control and completely free from repercussions. It also allows you to store that expression for safekeeping and ready access, which can be uniquely reassuring. Moreover, writing allows you to gain an understanding of the pain and its origins, and to even turn that pain into something beautiful.

Containment

A person's trauma is, in a way, valuable to them. It holds an ineffable significance. It's at one time something they wish they could escape, but at the same time, it's so personal, so informs who they are, that they cling to it. Frankly, I'm just as terrified to forget the things that have happened to me as I am to remember them. I need to remember what happened, and how it changed me, to distinguish the scar tissue from what's native to me. In many ways, a central part of my existence is to serve as a reservoir for painful memories.

My writing gives me a place to put them. I can unburden my soul by pouring them onto a page. I know, then, I'll never lose that essential part of myself, but that from this day forward I don't have to work to contain and conceal it within me. Having a place to put the hurt is a wonderful form of pain relief. To bury it down inside is to carry around some pollutant which is sure to bubble up time and again in insidious and unseen ways. To try to rid ourselves of it entirely is something like trying to claw away your skin—it's a part of you. Instead, we can put it here, on this humble page, for safekeeping.

Conversion

My favorite songs are all sad songs. There's something of the texture of existence in them; they're full to the brim with the experience that is life. They're about pain and heartbreak, weakness and failure, but they never make me feel sad. To hear about sorrow is something very different from actually experiencing it, so the pain encapsulated within the lyrics becomes something else entirely. The same thing happens when I put my own trauma into writing.

Suffering is nothing but ugly in the moment. It's pain, pure and simple, and there's almost nothing of art in it. However, when it is mollified and contextualized within a narrative, it is able to retain that deep poignancy without the overwhelming discomfort of its direct experience. Suddenly, pain becomes beautiful.

We can't look directly at the sun, but we can take in a picture of a stunning sunset for as long as we'd like. Embarrassing and unfortunate mishaps can bring us to tears if they catch us in a fragile state, but they invariably make for great stories down the line. Some things are too overpowering in full—they block out the beauty—unless and until their potency is reduced by an eventual conversion into art. It's this process that transforms tragedies into treasures. It's this process that allows one to turn trauma into something beautiful.

Confession

The blank page is a self-contained void. It's its own little world. I can put whatever I wish here and nothing will come of it. I can burn it. I can hide it. I can lock it away until the day I die. It's my possession, and my creation, and since only I know what it is I would put on it, no one else can compel me to do so.

There is so much I'd like to express. I'd like to tell some people I hate them; I have to regularly convince myself to allot those individuals the basic measure of forgiveness we're all deserving of. There are some people who I love more than anything, and I'd jabber on endlessly about how deeply I care for them if I wasn't wary of repelling them. But here, on this ever-heeding page, I can say all of it without any concern over the consequences.

In writing, I have exposed the first person to deeply traumatize me. I've expounded on why I had to stop talking to my mother. I've discussed how it felt to spend all of the years of my life bottled up behind a wall of social anxiety. I've delved into the frustration and trepidation I experience as a writer. I've discussed how my trauma has made feel so deeply unclean that I imagine I'll never return to "normal." I did all of that, and I didn't get into a fight with my abusive stepfather, or into an argument with my mother, or embarrassed about my crippling anxiety, or hardly anything else. This is my pocket universe, and I am free to express here without consequence.

Control

I look back over the years, and I am haunted by my mistakes. If right now, I stomp my foot, I'll never be able to do anything else with that single second for the rest of my life. The moment will have forever been dedicated to that particular act. Life is lived in only one direction, and each moment is indelibly inscribed onto that eternal, immaterial tablet called "time."

I can't take back the words I've said to people or the things I've done. There is only one place I can go where every mistake is forgiven. The paragraphs you've just read over were once riddled with mistakes, but I was allowed back time and time again to cleanse each sentence of its errors, until at last it became something near my conception of perfect. The page is both absolutely permanent and impermanent. It remembers for just as long as it is asked to, and it forgives as soon as requested. I'll never be able to rewrite my life, but I can edit my story indefinitely.

Cartography

I recently wrote a story about the time I saw my mom's boyfriend overdose on oxycodone. As the narrative unfolded line after line, I created something other than a story: I created a map of my soul. As I wrote one line, I felt nothing; as I wrote another, my hand would quiver, and I could feel the stir of trouble inside. Here there was hurt, and there there was none. This I had come to terms with, and that I had not. Without realization, I was charting out my pain.

For the story, I had to transform people into characters. I had to understand them. I had to look at them, their weaknesses and motivations, their relationships with one another, and my relationship with them, all interwoven into the complex tapestry that is a narrative—representative of the complex tapestry that is life. My intention was only ever to tell a story, but was it not in practice an investigation? Did I not create a picture of those events which served to deepen my understanding of them?

To tell a story, you must put everything in its place. Like the melody of a song, each element enters and exits at a given time. It starts slow and rises to a crescendo. At the time in my life described in that story, things proceeded in just the same fashion: They started slow, then quickened, until tragedy struck. The story, like any true story, is only a model of reality. It is a verbal representation of living, breathing people following their wants and succumbing to their imperfections. It was nothing but chaos as it happened, but now it is something organized and ordered that I can hold in my hand. Those tragic days all ran into each other; frustration didn't take breaks at night, and sadness didn't wait to arrive each day at a set time. Here, however, the scenes are separated by paragraph breaks, and each feeling is housed in a single sentence. It makes sense here. I am able to understand it now like I never did before.

Conveyance

A key factor in writing's ability to heal is not in the act itself but in making the piece public after its completion. Once we have taken a painful experience and packaged it into a number of paragraphs, it becomes compartmentalized. It was once only kept, with much discomfort, in the storehouse of the mind. Now, it has been moved to a new container. The only thing left to do is give it away, and that's precisely how it feels to share it with the public. One no longer feels the same need to remember what happened; the page assumes that role. One no longer needs to dwell on it; others will experience it instead, and in a very different light. It is gone from me, and that's all that matters. Trauma comes with a quiet responsibility. We feel obliged to keep it alive for the reasons earlier mentioned. By releasing it into the world, others come to keep it alive for us, and at no detriment to themselves. It is a wonderful rate of exchange that accompanies the conversion from anguish into art.

The audience's response augments this therapeutic effect. If the audience is kind and can relate, my pain becomes our pain. The weight of all things is lighter when the burden is shared, and the hurt each of us carries inside is no exception. Moreover, what may have once served to infuse an acidity and cynicism into one's personality when held within can act as a bridge for empathy and bonding when released. We see that our experiences are shared by strangers the world over, and that each of them cares for us by extension of the way they care for themselves, and wishes earnestly to ward off the suffering in our lives, just as they seek to ward of suffering in their own.

Symbolic acts are sometimes mirrored by real changes in the psyche. Therapists will tell their patients to write about their painful experiences on a piece of paper and then burn it. I have noticed a similar effect when making my writings public. The moment the button is pressed that makes the piece available to the world, a flood of emotions comes over you. There is nervousness, and a sense of accomplishment, but there is also a sense of relief: I held it in all this time, but now I have primmed and packaged it, and finally sent it to a thousand places far, far away from me.

Comfort

As hard as it is to write about our soft spots, it's almost always harder to speak about them. There were many years when, even with the people closest to me, I never felt I was able to speak on some of the subjects I've casually referenced here. In addition to all the ways writing itself has been freeing, it has also worked to loosen my tongue, by getting me more comfortable with these subjects.

Writing about these things can aid us in all the ways I've elaborated on throughout this piece. Putting ourselves before another soul and speaking about what we're carrying inside can do even more: It grows our capacity for intimacy. It knocks down the wall between one's self and everyone else. By strengthening our relationships, it further opens the door to all of what matters most in life—love and its fruits. Sometimes writing about our trauma is just the beginning.

Conclusion

When the world is cruel and life is hard, we often run to a sanctuary of sorts. While some people might spend time out in tranquil nature, or lock themselves in the confines of their bedroom, or travel to a far-off place, for writers there's only one place to go. It is a space of blank. It's an untouched space to call our own, to do what we will with. We can make it an ear to listen, a record to speak back to us, or a fire to toss whatever ugly thing into and let it go up in smoke.

Writing is my passion. It's also my career. More than anything though, it's my salvation.

In Conclusion

I worried at times that the overall message of this work, as it relates to a writer's career prospects, will come across as defeatist. I can never reduce writing to something as shabby as a means to popularity or money, so to characterize my thoughts as pessimistic on that score is somewhat besides the point. It is more than a means; it is an end in and of itself. However, if I were to hone in on that subject, I would refer the reader to another work of mine, *A Guide for Ambitious People.* In that work, I make clear my undying belief in the worth of grand ambitions, and would like to repeat here, unequivocally, that I encourage the unrelenting pursuit of your ambitions, whatever they may be. If you wish to earn all the world's riches solely by writing, then there is a way—and you should chase it hungrily. But the highest currency of life is happiness, and the true power lies in eternity. A writer sitting in a quiet room, content to create something masterful, even if they'll never live to see it applauded by the masses, is a force set to move the world in ways unmatched by the greatest and grandest of leaders and inventors history has ever known. Real power has always been silent, eternal, and immovable. This power is no exception.

Notes

Why Writing Takes Courage

1. "A Smooth Sea Never Made a Skilled Sailor." *Wiktionary*, 21 Oct. 2022, https://en.m.wiktionary.org/wiki/a_smooth_sea_never_made_a_skilled_sailor.

2. Harper, Douglas. "Etymology of masochism." Online Etymology Dictionary, https://www.etymonline.com/word/masochism. Accessed 13 July, 2022.

Why the People Closest to You Might Not Love Your Writing

1. Drake. *Care Package*. OVO Sound and Republic Records. 2019. CD.

2. Oscar Wilde, *Lady Windermere's Fan*

3. Friedrich Nietzsche, *Thus Spoke Zarathustra*

How to Deal With Being a Broke Writer

1. Kanye West. *Graduation*. Def Jam Recordings and Roc-A-Fella Records. 2007. CD.

Is It Egotistical to Post Your Writings

1. Tracy, Larissa. "The History behind Cersei's Walk of Atonement on Game of Thrones." *Longwood University*, 11 June 2015, http://www.longwood.edu/news/2015/the-history-behind-cerseis-walk-of-atonement/.

Why Your Writing Might Be Too Good to Be Popular

1. Ralph Waldo Emerson, *The Essential Writings of Ralph Waldo Emerson*

Why You Should Care Less About Your Writing

1. "9 Irish Blessings We Love." *Emerald Heritage*, https://emerald-heritage.com/blog/2017/9-irish-blessings-we-love.

Why Reading Is Essential for Writers

1. Ralph Waldo Emerson, *The Complete Essays and Other Writings of Ralph Waldo Emerson*

2. Stone, Robert, et al. "The Reason for Stories, by Robert Stone." *Harper's Magazine*, 1 June 1988, https://harpers.org/archive/1988/06/the-reason-for-stories/.

3. "Did One Man Write the First Great English Dictionary All by Himself?" *Dictionary.com*, Dictionary.com, 19 Jan. 2021, https://www.dictionary.com/e/johnson/.

4. "English Language." *Wikipedia*, Wikimedia Foundation, 9 July 2022, https://en.m.wikipedia.org/wiki/English_language.

5. Ralph Waldo Emerson, *The Essential Writings of Ralph Waldo Emerson*

Made in United States
Orlando, FL
27 December 2022